Stephan Szugat

Feel Great:

It's Your Decision!

How To Change Your Feelings By Deciding How YOU Like To Feel

Bibliographic Information of the German National Library: The German National Library listed this publication in the German National Bibliography; detailed bibliographic data are available at the dnb.dnb.de website.

Printing and Publisher: BoD - Books on Demand, Norderstedt, Germany

1. Edition
Print-ISBN: 9783754305270
eBook-ISBN: 9783754304563

Cover design by Stephan Szugat based on the image abstract-background-5185688 by AbdulStudio https://pixabay.com/images/id-5185688/.

Picture Courtesy for pictures and illustrations edited or not created by the Author of this book:

The image twister-303892 found at https://pixabay.com/vectors/twister-tornado-typhoon-spiral-303892/ was used as basis for the Emotional Scale Twister graphic created by Stephan Szugat.

Disclaimer

The author and publisher of this book and the accompanying materials have used their best efforts in preparing this book.

The author and publisher make no representation or warranties with respect to the accuracy, applicability, fitness, or completeness of the contents of this book. They disclaim any warranties (expressed or implied), merchantability, or fitness for any particular purpose.

The author and publisher shall in no event be held liable for any loss or other damages, including but not limited to special, incidental, consequential, or other damages. As always, the advice of a competent legal, tax, accounting, or other professional should be sought.

The author and publisher do not warrant the performance, effectiveness, or applicability of any idea listed in this book. All links are for information purposes only and are not warranted for content, accuracy, or any other implied or explicit purpose.

The material provided in this book or any related materials are for educational purposes only. The author and publisher are not providing any psychological service and this is not a recommendation about any kind of treatment or therapy.

Table of Content

Introduction

What You Could Get from This Book

This book is about How and Why to get into High Energy yourself to feel great.

Of course this book will also tell you how to STAY in High Energy as well as the Downsides of it and the Benefits it has for you and others.

It is not about Positive Thinking, not about Motivation or Mindfulness. Even not Meditation or Mindset.

Furthermore, this book has nothing to do with Esoteric or out of this World ideas. Not at all. It is based on my own experiences.

And even though you do not know me yet, you could trust me that I do not like these crazy up in the sky stuff as well as these "You can make it too"-Blabla.

Introduction

I have been with many motivational events in the past, where they told everyone to dance around and clap hands because you are the greatest.

A few days out of the event and you are back to "normal life". I guess you know what I mean. You get supercharged on these events, but no one tells you how to keep up your high energy.

Especially when the next bad thing happens or even when nothing happens for a longer period of time.

Though, I was always looking for something more sustainable. Interestingly, when you observe yourself and try many different things you find out much more than others could tell you about yourself.

It is all about how to manage your energy – and as a result, you might also positively influence the energy of people around you.

Okay, we will look into Self-Awareness which is also a thing you do with Mindfulness and other approaches. Yet, you still focus on energy using the exercises in this book.

Oh, I did not mention that so far, yes, there are exercises in this book. And it is a very good idea to do these exercises again and again.

Don't worry, they are easy and only need a little bit of your time. You might be done with an exercise in less than a minute, but you could even take much more time for it, if you enjoy it.

Therefore, the exercises are not time-intensive. That is because I do not like time-intensive things either.

Furthermore, it is easy to integrate the exercises into your daily life. However, you will find out that it is a good idea to increase your awareness about your feelings and thoughts.

Self-Awareness is one of many approaches. It is totally up to you which approach you chose. Choose an approach that resonates with you. One which you feel comfortable with.

With staying in High Energy you are going beyond Positive Thinking or changing your Mindset.

Last but not least, you may find out that I repeat things here and there. This is not an accident, this is by purpose.

And it is not to fill up this book, it is about to remind you. We learn by repetition. You learned to walk by repetition.

Anything you ever learned was by repetition. You repeat things again and again until you experience "Ah-Ha, now I got it". It's the same with the topic of this book.

Here is a quick summary of what you could get from this book:

► How to get into High Energy
► How to stay in High Energy
► Exercises to do the above

What Is In It For You?

As already mentioned there are simple methods for you to lift yourself up.

But most important are the benefits you could reap for yourself and others. Why for others? Why not? I explain it in a moment.

First, let's see what is in it for you personally. Here "personally" means all areas of your life. You could not improve one area of your life without benefiting other areas as well.

You may end up with more clarity about what is happening inside of you. That's not all. You may gain more clarity about what you want from your life. Which in turn could lead to better decision making. You could also gain more clarity about your relationships. Or even improve your relationships.

And of course, you will feel more powerful or even empowered. There is a chance that you may know some of the concepts I describe in this book. But maybe the context in which I present it to you will be new or different for you.

Though, hopefully, you gain insights into the interconnections that we all have to each other as well as the psycho-physical interconnections within us.

That brings me back to the benefits for others. Well, it might be that other people benefit when your energy gets higher and higher as well.

How could this be? You feel better, therefore you may act more loving, more polite, more peaceful. And much more. That is a gain for others as it is easier to get along with you. That does not mean others are allowed to walk over you.

Your relationships may get better, which is a benefit for everyone you have a relationship with. And that could be an awful lot of people. That is great. Imagine everyone loves to be around you and/or likes to do business with you. I agree that is a nice picture, but it might not happen.

There will always be people which may not like you. It's okay, we do not need to like everyone and we do not need to please everyone.

Accepting this truth helps your relationships too. Wanting to be everyone's cup of tea is an unreachable goal. Others might be more okay with you when your energy is high.

But that is not the point here. It's not about making you being loved. It's all about making you aware of the tremendous power and energy that is inside of you.

Don't believe me? Check it out for yourself. Though, what is in it for You? Or differently said, what are the benefits you could get from this book:

▶ gain clarity of what is happening inside of yourself

► gain clarity about which decisions to make (better decision making in business and life)
► feel better for yourself (happier, more confident)
► improve relationships with others
► more freedom for yourself and others
► simple methods to increase your energy level
► recognizing how much energy you have to achieve your goals.

What You Won't Find In This Book

This book is not about scientific proof. Therefore I will not provide any proof by mentioning any kind of studies.

That is because there are so many studies out there, which may prove my point of view and others that may not. Thus studies are a good option for discussion and going even deeper into the topic if you are interested.

However, for me it is more important to help you to experience what this book is about. Studies would help you to intellectually know what I'm talking about.

But your own experience is much more important. Also your own experience brings you the true knowledge which goes beyond intellectual knowledge.

The best way to prove things to yourself is to allow yourself to experience them. But remember, what ever you do has consequences. Therefore this book is about your inner experiences.

In case you are interested in more background research – into what I am calling 'high energy' - feel free to search the internet. You will find many interesting studies.

Another thing you won't find in this book is a secret or a quick tip. This is because there are no secrets about the topics covered in this book. There are different approaches to high energy. But a quick tip or quick way to do it, is not there either.

You have to do things more often to see results. That of course does not mean things are going to be hard. They might seem hard to do, but you could do it anyway as the methods I show you are simple.

Yet, you have to do it yourself. You have to use the methods described in this book. No one else can do it for you.

To summarize what is not in this book:

▶ reference to any scientific studies
▶ no secrets or quick tips
▶ information about any kind of shortcuts

A Little Bit About Myself

In my life I have gone through a lot of pain for not being good enough, not being successful enough, not having the life I wanted to live, being angry, being ashamed, being offended by whatever people said.

Introduction

I guess this may sound familiar to you as many people have kind of similar experiences in life.

Yet, the Methods and Techniques I share with you in this book, helped me gain insights, which have helped me get through all these emotions and setbacks.

All I tell you in this book is from my own experience.

However, this book is not about me, it is about your experience. That's the most important lesson I learned in my life. If you experience it, you know it.

Otherwise it is nice that you know, what I have gone through, but how is that helping you to find your own answers, your own energy source? It only helps you as I could direct you to where you could find it.

Therefore I keep the story about myself very short.

I got into Self-Improvement and Positive Thinking when I was about 17 years young. Since then I have tried and used many different methods, finding out that most of them are just too tedious or time-consuming to apply every day.

Back then there was no one talking about getting or staying in High Energy. Everything was all about Self-Improvement - meaning to change yourself to be a better person.

It was mostly about thinking in a different way.

Honestly, that takes a lot of energy. Most of the thoughts we have every day are negative. Just check it out for yourself by observing your thoughts.

In the years I started it was more of an esoteric movement. However, there have been lots of approaches that had been based on science already, but extremely hard to integrate into your daily life.

Fast forward, during the last 19 years I had been working as a Business Management Consultant especially for Finance and Accounting which gave me many opportunities to talk to Entrepreneurs, Business Owners and Executives and recognizing how important it is for them to have easy and effective tools.

Not that you need to be someone like them. No, what applies to these people, applies to every one of us.

No one likes to spend much time changing things. Me neither. Unknowingly I was searching all the time to find something simple and easy to implement in my daily life.

Whenever someone was interested I might have given some tips on what they could do for themselves. This way I always had a reason to continue my search.

For me being solution-focused is key. What I learned during my life and watching the lives of others is, that there is a solution to any problem/issue, if you are willing to look for it and use it.

Introduction

It might take a while for you to find/see the solution, but it is available. Maybe not right now. Keep going until you have it.

That should be enough about myself, let's get you to experience higher energy. Let's go.

My story in bullet points:

▶ have had tough times as all humans.
▶ started with Positive Thinking and other Approaches at the age of 17.
▶ most interested in simple approaches which are easy to implement into daily life.
▶ being solution-focused.
▶ always willing to learn.

The Amazing Power Of Staying In High Energy

Did you ever felt uplifted when someone was with you who had been on fire for something? I guess you had such an experience.

At least once in your life you did, even if you might not remember anymore.

Here being on fire means that this person was glowing from within, totally immersed into the chosen topic or task. No matter what, this person stayed on top of whatever came their way.

You may have wondered where this person took all this power from. Well, the answer is quite easy. They took all the energy from within. Even if they did this unconsciously.

Most of us may say "I don't have such a great power" or "I couldn't be so enthusiastic about something". Really? I believe you had at least once in your life something you had been enthusiastic about.

But something made you stop along the way to achieve it or to keep going at it. We are not looking back into that with this book.

It's more important that you recognize, that yes there was something I was totally on fire for. To get back to the point, being in higher energy feels good and it has many benefits for you and for everyone around you.

Though, what are the benefits for you? You feel great. That alone is a great gain. You are more peaceful, more accepting, more positive. Furthermore, you get things done more easily, though you are more productive.

That's not all. Being in higher Energy is also good for yourself as you are less stressed and your health will benefit from it. As if that would not be enough, being in higher energy also benefits your environment, which means everyone around you. Maybe even everyone in the world to some extent.

To tell the truth, we humans seem to have not yet fully understood how interconnected we are on all levels of life. If we would understand, we would stop harming each other, even with words.

Even Science is catching up on it, especially in Quantum Physics there had been interesting new theories or assumptions about the energy we are.

For the purpose of this book, we will just look at the amazing power of staying in higher energy and explore our own Experiences rather than diving deeper into scientific theories.

The experience you have for yourself is much more important than reading about it in any book or hearing about it from someone else.

> Just imagine being joyful, peaceful, and calm all the time and getting the things you want to be done with ease. Does that feel great? I guess it does. Did you recognize the little exercise you just did? I asked you to imagine being joyful, peaceful, and calm.

You couldn't imagine being it, without being it. Interesting, right? Thus you could not imagine how to feel, you just feel it.

Now, how are you going to feel that way all the time? Together we will take a look at it and examine the options. But first, we need to look at some other things as well.

For example, we have to look at letting go of feelings/emotions. Letting go of a feeling/emotion is similar to letting go of a pencil you hold in your hand. You just drop it. With feelings, it is the same principle, yet you could not see your feelings or touch them.

Therefore you have to connect to a feeling/emotion you like to let go and decide to drop it. That is all you need to do. When you feel a bit lighter you know that you dropped the feeling/emotion.

If you are a more visual person you could imagine energy of the feeling to evaporate through your skin or flow out at the sole of your feet. There are so many different approaches possible here. Just do it the way you feel most comfortable with.

How Your Energy Level Influences Your Decision Making Ability

Every one of us has had the experience, that decisions you make in a bad mood may not bring the results you really wanted.

And even worse, they might even harm you later. And "later" could even mean years later.

On the flip side, if you made decisions from a higher, more positive energy the outcomes are better and last even longer (at least most of the times that's the case).

This is something I observed so many times. Not only with myself, but also with others.

Deciding out of Fear is concentrating on what you don't want. Sure, you decide to get away from this fear.

At first, it looks like everything is okay. Later, something happens which may even not seem to be related to your prior decision that results from this fearful decision.

Again, you do not need to believe me. Investigate your life. Have you ever decided in a bad mood? We all did.

How was the outcome? Was it good? Did anything happen later, maybe years later, where you regret that past decision?

20

It wouldn't be any surprise to me. Yes, there will always be decisions you feel kind of nervous or uncertain about. They usually have this Uh-Oh-Feeling with them. Hope you know what I mean.

Regardless, it will be easier to make any decisions, when you are in higher energy. It does not mean that the nervousness or uncertainty disappears. You are just more okay with these feelings.

Now check about decisions you have made from a very good feeling. What do you remember? I guess there wasn't any backfiring event later, not even years later.

And I guess you felt great and have had a kind of certainty to your decision. Even if you couldn't tell why you are so certain.

In case there was something firing back at you, then it might have been not as harmful as with decisions made out of a bad mood.

At least that is my own experience.

Here is another thing how your energy level is influencing your decision-making ability. When your energy level is low by being in a bad mood like fear or hesitation, there is a sort of a foggy feeling.

It feels like you could not form a clear thought, yet you are aware of everything that happens. You may even feel numb or paralyzed.

Making good decisions out of such a state is hard. Maybe even impossible.

With the methods shown in this book, you have the chance to pull yourself out of such a mood and make your decision from a better place.

You do not need to wait until you feel good to make decisions, you could actively turn around your mood.

Turning around your mood takes courage, willingness, and determination. It's not happening by itself. You have to decide and go with your decision.

It's a simple thing, yet sometimes not so easy. You and I know that.

So here are the most important reasons why your energy level influences your decision-making ability:

- ▶ Decisions made from a bad mood could backfire on you even years later.
- ▶ While in a bad mood you may feel foggy, numb, or paralyzed, which aren't good states to make decisions from.
- ▶ Better decisions could be made from higher energy levels.
- ▶ You just feel great when your energy is high.
- ▶ You are in the "flow" when your energy is high. That means things are just flowing more easily - and even if things don't seem to flow easily, you can still feel relatively calm and accepting.

How Your Feelings Affect Your Energy Level

Your feelings have a direct connection to your Energy Level. If you feel depressed, you do not like to do anything. If you feel excited, you feel ready to take on everything. You probably experienced it yourself. If you feel down, it's hard to get started and to get anything done. When you feel great, everything just flows with ease.

Yet, it does not have to be the case that a bad mood, depression, or negative emotion has an impact on your energy level. This is because wecan examine the cause of the bad mood or the negative emotion.

Mostly you will find out, that it is a feeling you have that might not be related to the present moment. Now you have the power to overwrite anything the mind brings up as a feeling. Your power to overwrite the mind is in your decision. You could decide to follow the negative thoughts and feelings or you could decide to let them go and be positive no matter what.

Yes, this might not be easy all the time. However, it is very simple. You decide and you stick with your decision. If you plant a tree you don't dig it out after an hour just because you don't see any progress.

If you decide to be positive and more negative feelings come up, you can decide again to be positive. And you can do it again and again and again. Until you are feeling more and more positive.

You are not the slave of your feelings. You are the master of them! You allow yourself to experience them or let them go and be positive.

How you let go of a feeling is something you know from your childhood. You may have just forgotten how to do it consciously. Keep on reading, we will look into letting go of your feelings later as well.

It is not about suppressing your feelings by being positive or overwriting them, it's more about accepting them and deciding to feel different. Accepting your feelings might be the hardest thing to do when you really feel down. However, it is still your decision to feel down. So you might not have decided to accept and let go.

> Let's do a little experiment so that you get a better understanding of what I mean. Think of something that pulls you down. What do you experience? Doesn't feel nice, right? Think of something nice that pulls you up? Does that feel better? Who has decided on what to focus on? It was you, right? I just gave you an exercise again, but you decided to do it.

Did you need to suppress the bad feelings? No, you just decided to change your focus and felt better. Isn't that easy?

However, it takes practice and persistence to make these decisions all over again. It takes your effort and willingness to continue, no matter what happens around you.

It is your decision and you could only decide on one side of the coin. That is either being negative and feeling bad or being positive and feeling good.

You could not feel good and bad at the same time. Okay, that is not always correct. Sometimes we feel good and bad at the same time. I call it mixed feelings.

It might be that you are excited about something new and at the same time, you feel nervous or anxious about it too. When you get aware of the nervousness or anxiety you could do something about it. You let it go and focus on the good feeling.

Now, let's go and check out how your feelings affect your energy level.

Here is another example. When you get out of bed in the morning and you feel down. How is your day working out then? I guess it would not go as well as it could. You and I know how these days feel. It is so much you find you could hate about yourself.

It seems to be an endless stream of self-hate and disapproval. And on top of that, we also start to make others wrong.

Just check, how productive are you these days? Is your energy level high or low? It's probably low. And you do not see any chance to change that.

However, these are all just feelings and stories in your mind. You listen to them and give them life.

When you just stop doing that, you might experience how you feel better already. When you start giving yourself positive energy, you will get much lighter and feel even better.

You might also have had the experience that your day started like described above, but something happened during the day and your mood changed.

From that moment your day unfolded nicely. Have you ever investigated what has made you switch your mood?

If you did or not, does not matter right now. You could do it right now. Just remember such a day. Look for the moment where your mood changed.

What do you recognize? Did something happen that made you change your decision about how you feel? I guess that has been the case.

Another example of how your feelings affect your energy level: Imagine listening to your favorite music. How do you feel? Got the vibe?

Great. Now, would you say you feel higher than before, just because you listen to your favorite music? Hopefully, your favorite music is full of positive vibes.

In case your favorite music tends to be melancholic, well, that's not gonna bring you into high energy. It's more likely to pull you further down.

Which does not mean that it is bad to listen to such music. Sometimes I like such music too. But if you like to get into high gear, you like to listen to something positive and vibrating.

I, for example, love to listen to some kind of Pop Rock, Soft Rock, or other music with a high beat. Right away I feel much better. Though, by now you should have a clear understanding of how your feelings affect your energy level.

This does not mean your feelings are bad or problematic. They are just feelings and you are in charge to decide if you like to follow them or do something different.

Okay, another example of the effect of feelings. Have you ever had a situation where another human being pissed you off? If not, you are so lucky, hope you know that.

Well, but most of us did. How is your day evolving after an incident when you felt a lot of anger? Have you been productive? It depends, right? Maybe you can channel your anger into your work and get rid of it that way. Otherwise, it might not have been such a nice day, I guess.

Anyway, you got the point again. You are not the anger. You could follow the anger or you decide to let go of the situation and move on.

As a child, you did that many times, without remembering it. Now let's take a closer look at where these feelings - that affect your energy level – actually come from.

Below you find an image that visualizes how feelings affect your energy level and your life.

Again it's not about making anything wrong. We are talking about human conditioning here. From my point of view, it is relatively simple.

Yet it's not easy to get out of the cycle of human conditioning from one moment to the other. But it might be possible when we get a better understanding of how feelings and thoughts work.

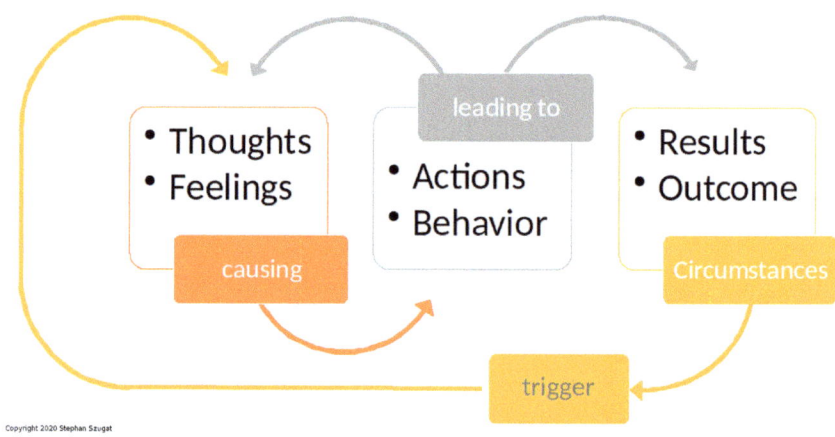

Take a look at the image above. You see "Thoughts & Feelings" which are causing "Actions & Behaviors" which in turn lead to "Thoughts & Feelings" as well as "Results & Outcomes".

The "Results & Outcomes" are the circumstances created from the "Actions & Behaviors" you have shown.

Then the circumstances trigger more "Thoughts & Feelings" and the cycle starts all over again.

This cycle runs 24/7. Even while you sleep. In this book, we use "Feelings" to bring you into higher energy. Why is that? Well, as you could see above, your feelings are kind of a root cause of what you are doing and what your results might be.

The impact is the highest with your feelings. Feelings even have a stronger impact than your thoughts. That is why you need a lot of positive thoughts to change things, but way less positive feelings to do the same.

Don't believe me. Just check it for yourself. Is the feeling of fear stronger, or the thought of fear? Do you simply THINK of "fear", or do you also FEEL it? Sometimes the feeling of fear can make us feel as though we are about to die - regardless of our rational thoughts. Also, this is proof to yourself that your feelings are more powerful than your thoughts.

BTW, thoughts and feelings play together. They usually don't occur separately. A thought is something like a concept or idea about something. Depending on the concept or idea about something we may experience different feelings.

There might be ideas that make us feel good, while other ideas or concepts about our life may make us feel bad. The mind works in pictures, it can't understand words. Here is a test of that: Think of a Horse. Has your thought been H o r s e or did you have a picture of a horse in mind? I assume it was the latter one.

Enough of the detour into the mind. Let's get back to the topic here again. Now you can probably better understand why positive music has an impact on your feelings and therefore on your energy level.

From the higher energy level, you get into, you are more likely to perform the right Actions thus having Results that you love.

Many of the thoughts and feelings we have are subconscious, which means you are not always aware of why you act in a certain way. If you notice any automatic behavior, just stop for a moment.

When you stop even in the middle of an automatic behavior you are on the way to change it. But that is not our topic.

To summarize how your feelings affect your Energy Level:

▶ feeling negative is equal to low energy levels.
▶ feeling positive is equal to high energy levels.
▶ feelings are more powerful than thoughts.
▶ thoughts and feelings often arise together.
▶ there are many ways to pull you out of a bad mood.
▶ to stay in a bad mood is your decision (every moment).
▶ you are in charge of how you feel.

Your Energy Level And Productivity

When your energy is low you are much slower than you used to be. Your thinking might be slower, your reactions might be slower. And it takes longer to get things done. Even the routine things.

With low energy, you may recognize that it takes longer to understand things. Even following a conversation might be more effort than usual.

You could observe something like that when you remember having headaches. You may recognize that everything feels drawn-out.

While you are having headaches your workflow is slower as well. This is different from when you feel on top of everything. Then your workflow might be smooth and everything goes easy through your hands.

Ever had such a day, where everything was in a harmonious flow and things magically got done? You may have wondered at the end of the day, "How have I done that? Accomplishing so much on a single day.".

Well, that is being in the flow of higher energy. You could create this kind of "flow" for yourself again and again. However, you could not force it. No, then it's not gonna happen.

How do I know? Well, I tried to force it so many times. Yet, when I'm not forcing it, it works the best.

Don't worry, I'm going to tell you exactly what I'm doing. It is so easy, I'm sure you can do it as well.

It only takes your decision and determination. But it does not need any kind of willpower.

Also, it does not need any extreme thinking effort. That's counterproductive as well.

A distraction-free environment could help but is not needed either. When you immerse into something totally, it doesn't matter what is happening around you.

Okay, here are some points about Your Energy and Productivity:

- ► When feeling low any task takes more time.
- ► When feeling high/good any task is much faster done.
- ► Being in high energy you could react faster (physically and mentally).
- ► more harmonious workflow with higher energy levels.

How High Energy Is Irresistible

High Energy is contagious. Don't believe me? Here is proof.

Have you ever been in a group of people when someone started laughing from deep inside and everyone started laughing too?

Yes? That was contagious high energy. True joy is high energy. If your answer was no, well let's see what we could do.

Maybe you had an experience where a person was enthusiastic about something, that their energy pulled you up as well. Or you just have been amazed by how much energy a person could have.

All this is high energy. Aren't you interested in why some people seem to have so much energy and others not?

If not, why have you bought this book? Seriously, you must have had a good reason to buy this book. If yes, that's great.

Let's examine anyway. And we examine this topic again by looking at ourselves.

Yes, why not? You may say "Oh no, I don't have so much energy as others". Really? How do you know? Did you ever try to have as much energy as others?

Remember what I said about knowing? Knowing by experience is the real knowledge.

Therefore let us find out how and where to find all this high energy. Here is the exercise:

Tapping into High Energy

Imagine doing something you really love. It must be something that brings a smile to your face, even when you are only thinking about it. Do you have anything? Great! Now allow this energy to come up that makes you smile about it. Do you feel you would like to do the thing right now? If yes, then that is the energy these people have all the time.

If you don't feel anything, it might be that the topic you were thinking about is not that interesting to you at this moment. Look for something that really, really brings up a good vibe in you. When you really chose something that you love and still could not feel the energy increasing, it might be that you are resisting or having fear about concentrating on that topic.

Accept the resistance or fear as it is. Allow it to be what it is, Energy. Relax into it. Then try again and allow the positive energy to come up.

Take a check, where did you find the energy that made you smile and want to do what you imagined? Inside of yourself, right? Of course, that's the only place where it could be.

How did you activate it? By just thinking about something you really love.

Now, this might be a clue here. You chose something that you love. Love is a very high energy, if not the highest in the Universe.

On the other hand, what are we all looking for? Correct, Love. All the time we are looking for Love. We could even say, everything we do is just because we are looking for Love.

Sounds crazy? It shouldn't, because it is all-natural. Just look inside yourself, there you could find the answer. Is this true? Love is not in your mind. It is in "You".

It does not matter how you define "You". From my experience and point of view, there is no way to describe "You". There is no way to describe something for which there is no word in our languages.

And you could not think Love. You could only experience Love. Loving something or someone with all of your heart is a very uplifting experience.

You never feel exhausted, when you love. Have you got an idea why high energy is irresistible? Yes? No? I tell you, though you know at least intellectually.

It is because you feel the love. Yes, it is that simple. Even if the person who you perceive as being in higher energy does not even know they are loving about a specific thing, subject, or person.

If you are following a fulfilling goal then you can't stop going forward.

It's not that you are pushing to go forward or forcing yourself to go forward. You just do it because you love it.

That's a different energy than just doing something to get around. However, you do not need to quit your job or throw away any kind of learning right now.

No, you dig into this love inside of you. You could even love the things you normally do not like to do.

Why not? It makes it much easier for you if you do things that you do not like with a smile on your face. The higher your energy gets the easier things might be for you. At least you feel great and others will recognize that.

And maybe they are much more willing to support you in your endeavors. Everyone likes to be around positive and loving people which motivate and inspire us.

Okay, I hear you saying "This is not me. I'm not this kind of person.". Again? Really? Well, you do not need to be someone out in the public to experience the irresistible impact of high energy.

You could experience it right where you are. Try it for yourself. Use the methods and exercises described in this book every day.
Whenever you remember, you give yourself more energy, more love.

Even if things might get worse, you keep going and give yourself more love and higher energy. It is your decision.

Why might things get worse? Have you ever used a broom to clean a dusty room? Remember what happened. You start sweeping and the dust goes everywhere.

Amazingly after you have finished, the dust settled and the room is much cleaner. But you had to go through the dirty phase and keep sweeping until the room was clean.

On the other hand, it might not happen to you that things get worse. Then you could call yourself lucky. The inner work you do with giving yourself more and more higher energy is changing things inside you and with that outside of you as well. It's inevitable. But you have to keep going.

Back to high energy being irresistible.

As already described earlier, high energy is irresistible as you feel good when you have it and when someone around you has it.

Energy is contagious no matter if it is positive or negative. Would you like to check that again? Don't believe what I tell you, prove it for yourself.

Okay, remember a situation in your life where you had been with a negative person. Maybe the person was telling you that everything is going downhill or something similar.

Have you felt how your energy got more and more negative? If we don't pay attention to our own energy level it's easy for others to pull us up or push us down.

But would you like to be a yo-yo? I guess not. And you do not need to be.

The little check you just performed on the negative energy, you could also do on positive energy.

Just remember a situation where you had been talking with someone where you felt better and better moment by moment.

Felt nice, right?

Now you might say that you could not choose who you are with all the time. That might be true. But you could choose how to feel all the time.

Why? Because you decide to follow the energy of the other people or the energy you decide to feel.

When you decide to stay positive, loving, and in high energy even while others talk and act negative, what do you think will happen?

Maybe nothing, maybe the others go away as they couldn't pull you down, or even better, they switch to positive energy as well.

Actually, it is not high energy that is contagious, it is that all energy is contagious. You just found out that this is the case by doing the little check I described above.

Hopefully, you did this little check. I couldn't do it for you.

As you know now that all energy is contagious, would you be more willing to focus on your own energy and keep it positive and high? Yes? That's great.

It might not be easy, yet it is simple.

Remember we talked about Self-Awareness earlier. It helps you to recognize your feelings and what happens around you.

From there you decide again how you like to feel. Keep focusing on the feeling you like to feel.

> You could even ask yourself "Could I feel even better?" You may answer with "Yes" or not at all. Find out which has more impact on how you feel, answering or not answering the question.
>
> Keep increasing your energy.
>
> Furthermore use your Self-Awareness to observe what happens around you, when you continue to increase your energy.
>
> At one point you might even ask yourself "Could I love even more?". I know the answer to that. Find out for yourself.

With this little experiment you have checked how energy is contagious. Also you might have heard many people suggest you should surround yourself with positive people.

That is a good idea, but it might not always be possible. You do not need the other positive people to feel better. It depends on your own decision to feel better.

Yes, it helps you to be among positive people to get out of a bad mood much easier. However, it is not that you couldn't do it yourself.

We humans tend to believe that someone or something has caused us to experience emotional reactions. And we also tend to believe we need others to get away from these emotional reactions again.

This may or may not be true. You have to investigate for yourself by taking a look inside to see if you may have been the cause of your experience.

The Emotional Scale Twister

But let's take a closer look at our Emotions. There are so many different theories about emotions out there. Some say there are seven basic emotions other even say there are more than 30 basic emotions.

As science is not yet clear about it, how can we be certain? We can't, but we could take a very simple approach, which will be good enough for us and the illustration here.

With the positive emotion, your energy goes up, with the negative it goes down. The illustration on the next page shows two twisters. One spiral is upward and one spiral downward.

These are the directions of your emotions, up or down. A twister is a great picture of our emotions as they are strong on the outside, but there is stillness in the middle of the twister.

When you investigate your emotions you find out, that even behind strong emotions is stillness. And even between strong emotions is stillness.

I named the positive twister "Love" and the negative "Hate". This is to make clear that you could not be both at the same time. Love is no emotion from my point of view. Love just is. The Love I mean here is unconditional. Anything different is not Love.

Unconditional Love is to love without wanting anything back for the love you give. Yes, that is radical, but that is what unconditional means.

Let's take a look at the Emotional Scale Twister now.

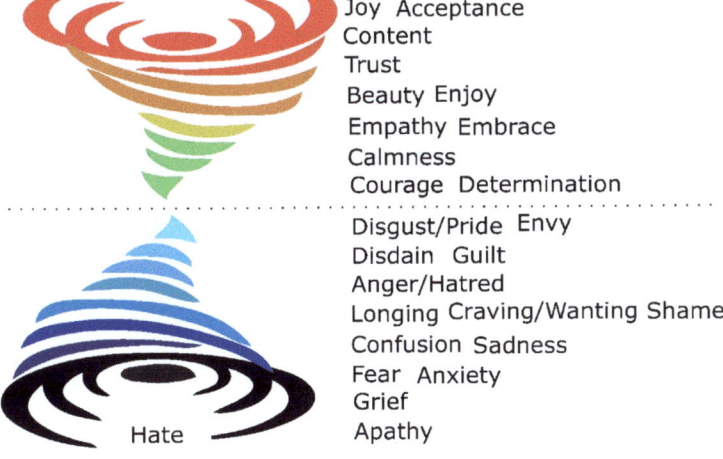

Love

Peace
Joy Acceptance
Content
Trust
Beauty Enjoy
Empathy Embrace
Calmness
Courage Determination

Disgust/Pride Envy
Disdain Guilt
Anger/Hatred
Longing Craving/Wanting Shame
Confusion Sadness
Fear Anxiety
Grief
Apathy

Hate

Please do not deem the list of emotions as complete, I just mention a few emotions to give you an idea. The negative, as well as the positive emotions, are on a kind of scale. Disgust/Pride is much higher energy than Apathy.

Peace and Acceptance on the other hand are much higher energy than Courage and Determination. You could examine any emotion yourself and place it on the scale. Just feel into the emotion and you know where it belongs on the scale. If you need any scientific background, search the internet. But don't get yourself confused by all the information you may find. Now you got a bit more background about your emotions as well.

Maybe the illustration above helped you to better understand why High Energy is Irresistible. Don't you think it's time to recap again? Yes, I think the same. Here we go:

▶ high energy is irresistible as it is contagious.
▶ we all like to feel good, therefore high energy is irresistible.
▶ all energy is contagious, no matter if positive or negative.
▶ you are the only one who decides how you feel.
▶ you could be in positive high energy even if negative people are around you.
▶ There is no need to be a yo-yo to the energy of others, you decide your energy.
▶ It's easy to increase your energy level as it only depends on your decision.

All Is Energy

I must warn you, as you might already noticed I may simplify things to make them easier to understand. Where ever possible I will make you aware that the situation might be more complex than it sounds.

However, if we really take a close look to life, it is actually very simple. Yet it looks very complicated when you see all the parts and their interconnections.

If you take any single item about life, you find out that it is in fact very simple, if you drill down deep enough.

As a matter of fact, if you drill down deep enough everything is energy. Yes, one of the smallest forms we know is an Atom. Maybe not if you drill down even further.

Anyway, an Atom has a core and a part that spins around the core. Between these two parts is a lot of space or nothing.

All is Energy

It is quite interesting. Okay, I described it very simply, but that's what I told you. Science had discovered decades ago, that atoms or particles act differently in an experiment if there is an observer present or not.

From the aforesaid we could conclude that energy is influencing energy. And as the observers had been humans, that implies we are all energy as well.

So far, so good. But I guess you knew this already. Now as all is energy you could imagine that if you send out negative or low energy, that only this low or negative energy could come back to you.

If you wish something good to happen in your life, you have to send out good energy. It's that simple. Yet, it is not always easy. Here is an example of what I mean. Years ago I was with a client. I shared an office with the accountant. We had a good relationship as coworkers.

Well, I was her supervisor, but as she did a great job I did not need to supervise her. Anyway, one morning when I got to the business again (I was only there once a month for a week or so), we talked about things that happened while I wasn't present at the office.

At one moment she started complaining that she has "this" problem with the ERP-System and nobody from the IT-Department came around for the last four weeks to fix it.

While she was telling me her story, I was giving her and the IT-Department some love. After 5 minutes one of the IT-Staff popped into our office and asked her that she had "this" problem with the company software and he would go and fix it quickly right now.

The look on her face just said "What the heck is happening here?". Her problem got fixed right that moment. If the word "Love" does not resonate with you, because you believe it has nothing to do with business then just replace it with "sending positive energy". Now, how have I done that? Any idea? It's easy. It really is. No idea?

Okay, let me explain though you could do it as well. First, you need to relax. It will not work when you try to force it. Could you relax a little bit more? Okay, good. Now create a nice feeling anywhere inside of you. For example a warm feeling in your stomach or so.

Expand this feeling until it fills more of your body. Now send it out beyond your body. There is no need to focus the energy on a specific person. You could do that. But it is not needed.

Just continue sending out this nice warm feeling. Witness what happens. Maybe nothing. Could that be okay for you? Maybe something you did not expect happens. Or that which you wanted to happen. Whatever it is that has happened or did not happen, what do you experience? I guess you feel better.

You see, even with such a little exercise you were able to shift your energy level.

All is Energy

Did you need to think a lot to change your energy level? Did you need to force it? Not at all. You decided and you did it. No thinking necessary.

Even if nothing happened from sending out the positive energy, you feel better by doing so. That's a tremendous gain.

Did you feel exhausted by sending out good, positive energy? No? Wow! Isn't that amazing? You send out good vibes and don't get exhausted. Another great gain, don't you think.

On the other hand, the above experience could tell you something about your true nature. You could not run out of energy. If you do, it's because you tell yourself that it is that way.

Just send out some more good, positive energy. What do you experience? Do you feel better again? How often could you do this simple exercise? You could do it all the time when you decide to do it and do it.

As all is energy, everything and everyone is interconnected. We do not see it clear all the time.

What you say is energy. What you think is energy. What you feel is energy. What you do is energy. What you eat and drink is energy. Whatever you use is energy.

Did I forget anything? Anyway, even if I have forgotten something, you got the idea. Even your expectations are energy, because your expectations ARE simply thoughts and/or feelings.

As all is energy even your feelings are energy and they have an impact on your life. And not only on your life. On the life of everyone. Not just your family and friends.

Your feelings have an impact on you and everyone!

Let's check this out. Did you ever feel a strong negative feeling out of nowhere? You might wonder, why the heck I feel this way. Your day might have started wonderfully.

Later during the day you might saw the news and you recognized something really bad happened in another part of the world, and many people felt sad or shocked.

In case you have not had such an experience, don't worry. Here is another way to check it out: You had a really good loving feeling about a specific person and maybe thought about calling this person the next day. All of a sudden, this person calls you.

I can't tell how many times that happened to me. Or something similar. Seemingly, we humans have not yet fully understood how connected we are with each other as well as the world and everything in it.

If we would have understood, we wouldn't harm each other or try to cheat and betray each other. But that's a different story.

Back to all is energy. Even your body is energy. And it is possible to measure it. Years ago I bought a device that could show the electric tension in my body.

All is Energy

It's very interesting. When I feel fear the energy is rising, but it is negative energy, even though it might be a strong one.

When I feel more love the electric tension goes up again, but this time it feels much better and is positive.

You do not need to buy such a device. I just bought it out of interest, but it was really expensive. Today you might get these gadgets much more inexpensive, smaller, and better designed.

Hopefully, you could understand more clearly now, that everything is energy. It might not be new to you to hear this. We tend to forget, when our life is not going our way.

Why not increase your energy level if things are not going your way? It's much easier than trying to force things to change.

Let's recap:

▶ Whatever is around you is energy.
▶ What you are is energy, which includes your body as well.
▶ every energy has an impact on your life.
▶ Your energy has an impact on everyone and everything in the world as well.
▶ What you say is energy. What you think is energy. What you feel is energy. What you do is energy. What you eat and drink is energy. Whatever you use is energy.
▶ Even your thoughts and feelings are energy.

How To Get Into Higher Energy In 4 Simple Steps

As said before, it is all about your decision. You probably heard a saying that "Life is a decision". In fact, you are making thousands of decisions every single day without noticing most of them. In this chapter we take a look at the steps you could take to lift yourself up. The method described here does not mean to be the only way to do it. It is what I found to be the simplest way for me.

Hopefully you find it is a simple and easy way for you too. In the previous chapter, we had been using a different approach, which is as powerful as the one you are about to read. It only takes four steps to get into higher energy and none involves thinking or willpower.

The Steps

1. Get aware of how you feel
2. Decide to be okay with how you feel
3. Decide how you like to feel
4. Feel the way you like to feel

As we know the steps now, let us explore them on a deeper level.

1. Get aware of how you feel

It is important to recognize how you feel. It is the first step of accepting the way you feel. By recognizing how you feel even if it is a bad feeling you are less likely to suppress the feeling.

Suppressing your feelings would be the opposite of what we are doing here. Being aware of your feelings means to start to accept them, no matter how horrible they might feel the moment you feel them.

2. Decide to be okay with how you feel

Being okay with how you feel is full acceptance, which means you do not want to hold on to how you feel or want to change how you feel any longer.

It is like saying "Yes" to the feeling. Which is also helpful to do. You could even ask yourself: "Could I be okay with the feeling I have right now?" and answer with Yes. You could do so until you feel more at ease and okay with the feeling.

Maybe the feeling disappears totally if you keep going with this process. Play with the question and the answer or non-answer.

What does that mean? Well, ask yourself "Could I be okay with the feeling I have right now?" and just don't answer the question.

We tend to give answers to questions, but who said it is necessary to answer questions we asked inside of us? I don't know. But it's amazing what happens when you are not answering the question. Try it for yourself. BTW, it might not be polite in a real conversation to not answer a question. But that's totally up to you.

3. Decide how you like to feel

This is an important step. Even with your feelings you won't get anywhere when you are not deciding where to go. This step is to decide to feel, calm, happy, joyful, peaceful, powerful, loving, or whatever it is you like to feel. It's all up to you. No one else could tell you how to feel.

You decide clearly about where to go with your feelings. Remember, it's not about suppressing the feelings you do not like. Accept the feeling you have first and then decide how you like to feel.

4. Feel the way you like to feel

With this step you go into the feeling you like to have. But pay attention to not trying to force the feeling. For example, you decide to be calm and allow yourself to feel it. There is no need to force yourself to feel calm.

It is crucial that you just allow the feeling to arise as you focus on it. At first it may take some practice to feel the way you want. But with time it gets easier and easier.

Here is a little trick that you could use. Let's stick with wanting to feel calm. While you concentrate on feeling calm, just say the word in your mind. Repeat it as often as you like, but don't overdo it. A few times should do it. And it is not something you do in a hustle.

Easy, right? Remember, normally there is no need to "think" yourself into the feeling you want to feel. Here we used thinking as a trick to be focused. The more you practice, the less you need to think.

Now I guess the four steps are easy to remember and to apply. But they will not work for you, if you don't practice them for yourself.

Though it is a good idea to remind yourself or to set a reminder for yourself. We all tend to forget about good things as soon as one little bad thing happens.

It reminds us about all these things that went bad. But normally there are also a lot of things that went well. Why not start focusing on the good ones more often? It's your decision.

If the four steps are even too much to remember for you, here is an even faster way. Just do step 4. Correct, just do this last step. Feel the way you like to feel.

Increase that feeling again and again. Simple? Yet, you have to do it again and again.

No one else could do it for you. And I assume it is so easy, that you could even have the feeling you like even while you do other things.

Okay, I know, it takes some practice. You could do it. Just keep going.

Another funny thing is, that when we feel good and things are going our way, we stop doing the things that helped us get to this point.

So be aware, to keep going further even if things are evolving in a way you want. Keep increasing your energy level.

It's Not About Motivation, It's About Lifting Up Your Energy

Motivation is one way you could apply to bring your mood up. But it takes a lot of energy sometimes to motivate yourself.

Also motivation is something you do with and in your mind. Motivation, from my point of view, also involves a lot of willpower. However, the mind is also where all these thoughts are that pull you down.

That's why it takes so much energy to reprogram your mind. You have to put more positive energy into it, than the amount of negative energy that is in there already.

By increasing your energy you will lift yourself up anyway. There are no thoughts needed to increase your energy.

There is also no willpower needed. It takes your decision, that's all. And you do not need to force good thoughts or good feelings into your mind. You just allow the energy to arise inside of yourself.

A little exercise again:

How do you allow the energy to arise within yourself? Well, let's go with joy as the feeling for this exercise you are going to increase.

Now invite the joy up within yourself, by just focusing inside and invite the joy to come up. Don't try to feel joy, just invite it up and observe.

If you try too much, you are forcing joy to come up. That does not work.

Keep observing. Does nothing happen? Okay. No problem.

Do the following. Ask yourself "Could I feel more joy?" and answer the question with "Yes". Ask yourself again.

Ask yourself again. And again. And Again. What do you experience? I guess you feel a little bit more joy than before you asked yourself if you could feel more joy.

It's interesting that just by asking, you could bring up good feelings. You may just feel a little bit of joy, but it proves it works.

To increase the level of joy you feel, just keep going with the exercise above.

Back to Motivation. Motivation is not a bad thing. However, too much importance is placed on it.

Everyone is telling you to keep motivating yourself, and that it is important. But the question is also, are you trying to overcome negative energy by increasing your motivation?

If the answer is yes then how much energy will that need to make something positive happen.

Honestly, it takes a lot of positive energy to overwrite the negative energy we all run around with. But that's not a problem that is ever attacked.

The negative energy inside of you will still be there no matter how much you motivate yourself. At one moment in your life, it will show itself again. Instead of throwing so much energy into motivating yourself, why not love yourself.

Don't like to love yourself? If not, why do you try to motivate yourself? Doesn't make sense to me. When you motivate yourself to do something then the question is if you are motivating yourself because there is something negative in your life that you want to change.

But you sabotage yourself by keeping your feelings on the negativity the whole time you motivate yourself. Subconsciously you might even fear that what you are doing does not work or you may lose everything again, when you achieved the change you wanted.

It's Not About Motivation, It's About Lifting Up Your Energy

Of course, lls you that you need to motivate yourself or you need to work hard to achieve your goals doesn't mean it's the only way to achieve something.

Yes, many people proved the point that hard work makes it possible to achieve your goals.

On the other hand, there are people which worked smart and achieved their goals as well. What kind of person are you? The hard worker or the smart genius?

Both are good, no matter which kind of person you are. It's not about "this or that" it is about "this and that". Use everything to the best of yourself and everyone.

Oh, I couldn't believe it, but I forgot to clearly define "Motivation" with you. Okay, sorry for that. As it came to me right now, let's define what "motivation" actually is. Do you agree?

Motivation is wanting to change something. That could be everything you are not satisfied with right now. It might be your fitness, your income, or your living situation. Even relationships.

You got the idea. As of the above motivation looks like a good thing as it includes persistence and willpower to do something about the thing you are not satisfied with.

But! There is a lot of negativity behind it, could you see it? If not, here is a hint. When you are not satisfied with something do you feel good about it? I guess not.

You feel you "need" something better or at least different. In other words, you believe you lack something. And you desperately want to have that missing thing. Still you "motivate" yourself to do something to get rid of this disturbing feeling of missing something or wanting something different.

That disturbing feeling is negative. You feel bad about something as it is right now. Great motivation from my point of view - to be a little ironic here.

Thus you motivate yourself by being negative and force yourself to be positive and do something about the negativity. You try to get something positive out of being negative.

Hmm, looks like a great effort. And it is, right? Ever tried something different? Imagine being okay with whatever is around you, what you have, what you are. be/have/do...".

Does that feel more positive? Don't get me wrong it is not about avoiding wanting something. That's okay.

It is to go for a change from a much more positive and open attitude. When you are more open and positive it will make the doing much easier and more effortless.

It's Not About Motivation, It's About Lifting Up Your Energy

Even if you have to do things regularly to see progress. Well, you could say that it is motivation as well. Good, for me it is more about being purposeful.

Being purposeful means that you have your goals in front of your eyes, yet you do not force anything to happen or force yourself to change something.

Yes, you do what is needed while still being open and positive. Being purposeful does not mean avoiding taking action.

Here is another way of saying what I like to say. Motivation sometimes or most of the time feels pushy. Just take a look at all the things which might come to your mind you need/want to change.

You want to change your thoughts, your feelings, your behavior, your environment, your relationships, or even your self-expression. Sounds like a lot to be motivated about.

You don't need to motivate yourself when you feel great. Do you? Of course not. You are already burning for the things you like to do. That is the difference to be in high energy. Your motivation is natural in high energy and not negativity-based as it is most of the time.

Right now, could you allow yourself to feel good? Just decide you could. And could you feel even better? And more? And even more? What do you experience now? Do you feel lighter? Do you feel more energized? Do you feel more interested in taking action now?

Did you need to motivate yourself to feel good? No, you didn't. You just decide and allow yourself to feel good.

Thus you do not need any motivation. Decide to feel good and you will feel good if you keep deciding until you feel good. And then you keep continuing to decide to feel good.

Sounds simple. Yet it isn't easy all the time. Be persistent with your decision, but remember not to force anything.

To recap:

► being in high energy has nothing to with motivation.
► being in high energy is a decision.
► being in high energy makes it easier and more effortless to do the things you want or have to do.
► being in high energy just feels great.

The Secret About Self-Awareness

Let me start with a question. Do you really believe there is a Secret about Self-Awareness? To be honest, from my point of view there is no secret.

You have Self-Awareness all the time. You may not pay attention to it. First we need to define what Self-Awareness really is.

Self-Awareness means you are cognizant of your feelings, your thoughts, your behavior, the world, and other people and lives. It also includes our reaction to our thoughts, feelings, and behavior,

It has nothing to do with improving your behavior or changing your feelings. But it is the first step to start with. We usually tend to use our Self-Awareness to fit into the world. To be accepted.

Self-Awareness might sound a bit magical, esoteric, or even complicated. It isn't the case as you have already read above. It is a natural ability every one of us has. And maybe even animals have it. Who knows?

The Secret About Self-Awareness

Isn't it interesting what we humans are willing to do to be accepted by others? However, this is unnecessary. If you like to feel good, don't wait until someone gives you some love and affection. You could give love and affection to yourself.

Yes, it is really nice to receive love from others. It isn't necessary to give yourself up for that. The more you love yourself, the more others may give you love too.

Back to Self-Awareness. My own experience showed me, that Self-Awareness goes far beyond the body's senses. And that has nothing to do with taking drugs. And it isn't needed for you to have beyond body experiences to feel great or stay in high energy.

You could use your Self-Awareness to get into higher Energy. By using the four steps described in this book, you already use your Self-Awareness.

As you are present to your momentary feelings, you are self-aware. Then you are in a position which you could use to decide, if you like to stay with the feeling you have or if you like to change it.

Thus it is always your decision how you feel and how you react. Self-Awareness helps you to recognize the power of your decision.

The only secret that might be there about Self-Awareness is to use it to ask the right questions to yourself and about yourself. Going from Self-Awareness to Self-Inquiry. There is one thing about Self-Awareness that is not recognized most of the time.

Self-Awareness is subjective. You could not be aware of yourself in an objective way, except you would be able to not think of and about yourself when you are aware of yourself.

The sense or view you have about yourself will always include thoughts and feelings. We might even disapprove of ourselves. We often ask ourselves "Why is/has…?". This type of question will lead you down into the abyss of the mind.

More helpful are questions starting with "What", "How" or "Who". The latter one shouldn't be used to search for someone to blame. Because when it comes to our life, it is each one of us to blame, not someone else.

Self-Awareness could also be translated to being in the moment and recognizing what is going on inside and outside of you without judging it. Feeling, Hearing, Seeing, and so on.

Some might say that's more about Mindfulness. Well, we humans tend to describe the same thing with many different words and methodologies. Neither is good nor bad – right or wrong.

We could agree on being in the present moment with our awareness without any judgment. That is for me Self-Awareness as well as Mindfulness. It's simple, yet, we all tend to make it more complicated than it is.

> Let's do an exercise right now. Take a deep breath in. Really deep start from the bottom of your belly up to your chest. Relax while you breathe in.

> Slowly breathe out. Keep breathing deeply in a natural flow. What do you recognize? Are there fewer thoughts? Do you feel calmer? Do you recognize more of what is happening inside and outside of yourself?

If your answers had been "Yes" to the above questions, wonderful. Now you experienced what it is to be more aware. If your answer was "No", try again. Take a deep breath and relax.

There is no need to be fearful about this exercise. Relax. Nothing could happen to you. Breathing deeply is more healthy as you get more oxygen into your body.

Even if your answer to the earlier mentioned questions is still "No", you are aware. Check if there are any feelings. Any wanting to have a certain experience, any expectation.

Self-Awareness has nothing to do with expectations or wanting. You just have it. The moment you recognize a thought, a habitual reaction, or similar you are self-aware.

It's easy and simple. It does not take any time to be aware. You are it, but you may have to bring your attention to it.

Oh, here is something you need to know about Self-Awareness, that might be a bit uncomfortable, but I mentioned it indirectly already. The more you get aware of your Self, the more you might notice negative thoughts and feelings.

Recognizing more negative thoughts and feelings could be disturbing, irritating, or even overwhelming.

Don't worry. Feelings and Thoughts are just energy. Relax into them and allow them to pass through. You wouldn't hold on to a cloud in the sky, right?

Give your feelings and thoughts the same freedom as you give a cloud. Allow them to flow through you. By staying relaxed even when a thought or feeling is overwhelming it will pass through.

If you feel that you tense up when a strong feeling or thought comes up, remember to relax into it. It might even help to say "Yes" to the feeling.

The moment you notice the feeling or thought you are aware. That means you are aware more than you think you are. Of course, there could be moments when you come back into the actual present moment and find yourself recognizing you had been unaware for a certain amount of time.

Don't disapprove of yourself because of it, it just happened. Be happy you are aware again. To even increase your Self-Awareness you could ask yourself the following questions. The list is not meant to be complete, these questions are samples. Play around with them and add your own:

► Am I aware?
► Am I loving?
► What am I experiencing right now?

The Secret About Self-Awareness

▶ What do I smell, taste, hear, feel?
▶ Am I peaceful?
▶ Am I relaxed?

Even though these are questions and you might be tempted to answer them, don't answer the questions. Let them answer themselves.

Concentrate on your experience rather than focusing on the mental process of answering the questions. What else could you do to increase your Self-Awareness? Most importantly, have a short moment again and again, where you focus on what is happening inside and outside of yourself.

Furthermore, you could use Meditations to increase your Self-Awareness. A good idea is also taking a walk and allowing yourself to recognize everything without thinking about it.

The latter takes some practice as you will see. The mind often comes in and tells you exactly what you see and hear and also some assumptions it calculates from the things it just commented on.

Don't mind it! Focus on your experience and allow everything else to flow through you. Though, now, do you still believe there is a secret about Self-Awareness? Or anything new about it?

Whatever your answer has been, just allow it to be gone and give yourself the freedom to experience Self-Awareness again and again.

There is no need to hold on to the experiences you have had so far. Be open to new experiences, be open to new levels of Self-Awareness.

Additionally, Self-Awareness has to do with recognizing how others see us. As we all try to fit in, this part might take a lot of energy.

Yet, we are afraid of stopping to please everyone else.

Stopping to please everyone else to fit in does not mean to become a rude and/or ignorant person.

It has more to do with the awareness that you already have the good energy inside of you thus you do not need to force others to give you something you believe you need.

Remember this book is about feeling great, staying in higher energy. Self-Awareness could help you to see that you want others to lift you up. That's not gonna work as everyone is doing the same thing.

Everyone is looking to be uplifted from you. In this case, start lifting yourself up first. Then you may decide to do your best to help others to lift themselves up.

The higher your energy gets, the more you help yourself and everyone else. Check it out for yourself. Do the work and find out what happens.

The Secret About Self-Awareness

So far so good. Let's recap again:

▶ there is no secret about Self-Awareness.
▶ you are Self-Aware all the time, you may not focus on it.
▶ Self-Awareness is about how you see yourself, how others see you as well as being aware of how you feel, act, think.
▶ Self-Awareness also has to do with being present to what is happening, thus you could interact more positively. Especially when automatic habits coming up.
▶ It's easy to develop and focus on your Self-Awareness, it only takes your decision. A deep breath might help as well.
▶ There is nothing you need to actively do to be Self-Aware. Being Self-Aware is much more passive, yet you could be very active when you are fully aware.
▶ Diving into Self-Awareness might bring up strong feelings. Good and Bad. Stay relaxed and they flow through you.
▶ Self-Awareness helps you to remember to stay in high energy.

The Role Of The Environment And Why It Doesn't Matter

Our environment in terms of the people around us have an impact on us. This is because we are much more interconnected than we believe and because we need social contacts as humans.

During the last chapter, we made an experiment to prove that already.

On one hand we like to be with other people, but on the other hand we don't. It depends on the experiences we have made in our interactions with others. Still, we could not get away from other people totally.

Therefore we have to find a way to deal with other people, even if they trigger intense feelings in us.

If you take a look at how we humans react to good things, you will recognize many people are quite negative about good things happening in their life. That might even be true if your energy becomes higher and higher.

The Role Of The Environment And Why It Doesn't Matter

Some people will use their best efforts to pull you down. Not because they don't like you to be in high energy and feeling great, but because they don't have it themselves. It's a subconscious habit we all have to a certain degree.

But don't believe me, check it for yourself. You could check it out by observing how others are reacting towards you when you are in high energy and feel great.

Most people may like it, but a few people who don't like it, could be enough to pull you down. Especially if these people are part of your family. Our family members can trigger us the most.

And you could not leave your family behind so easily. And that is even not necessary. This is because your family is not responsible for how you feel. You are!

Your family, friends, colleagues, or any other person may trigger bad feelings in you, but still, you are the one who feels them, thus you are responsible for your feelings.

When you investigate the topic, you find out, that it does not matter what others say or do to you. It only matters how you feel about it. And that of course is your decision.

Again, it is not about suppressing your negative feelings. Allow them to be as they are and concentrate on the feelings you want. Feel peaceful, feel joy, or anything you want. It is your decision. Now, what is the role of our environment? Well, let me put it that way, the role of our environment is to point us back to ourselves.

Here environment means everything and everyone around you, even the whole world at some point.

Pointing us back to ourselves means recognizing our internal reaction to the happenings in our environment and the world. Simple, right? Yet, staying in positive high energy is a simple task, but not always easy. It takes practice.

It is correct that it is easier to stay positive when you are among positive people. On the other hand, you don't have a choice all the time with whom you are together. It will happen that negative people are around you.

As said about our families. You couldn't get rid of them and you do not need to. Your family will recognize when you stay in high energy more often. And you will enjoy your family anyway no matter if they are negative or positive.

We all tend to allow the overall energy of a situation to influence us. But that doesn't need to be the case. Here is an example. Imagine being among many people enjoying a music event.

Even if you would join the event a little later than most people, you would immediately feel the good vibe at the event.

Now, when you join a group of people that are angry about each other and fighting verbally, you may have a different experience. It could be that you take part in the fight because of the energy you feel even though you might have been in a good mood before you joined the discussion/argument.

The Role Of The Environment And Why It Doesn't Matter

Here is a little story of how I came to see the above in our world. I was traveling to a big city where I had never been before. The first day I walked around in the area close to my hotel.

Fortunately, I booked a hotel close to the city center. While strolling around I bought myself some tickets for sightseeing tours. The next day I started with these tours. The last of the sightseeing tours had been in the late afternoon a few days later. Close to the end of the tour, the bus drove through a small road very slowly. All of a sudden I felt so bad and negative.

From everywhere I felt I was being bombarded with negative feelings. About 15 minutes later the tour ended close to a square in the city center. I nearly fell out of the bus as I felt like I was drunk. Yet, I only had water with me.

Still, I felt all this negativity. Fortunately, there was a skating rink in the middle of the square of the city center. I walked there and enjoyed watching the people skating. Within a couple of minutes, I felt much better and the bad feelings went away.

And I felt positive for the rest of the day. Since then something similar didn't happen to me again. Why? Because I decided to allow all energy to flow through me instead of holding on to it. Additionally, I decided to be positive and loving.

You see the role of the environment is not only negative. It could be both, positive and negative. But never both at the same time. However, it is always our choice if we follow the energy of the pack, meaning the energy of the majority of people.

It does not matter how many people are around you, to be in positive high energy is your decision. You may need to make that decision several times again and again.

Anyway, even though I repeat myself over and over again. Your environment does not determine your energy level or how you feel.

Your environment has an impact on how you feel, but you are the one who decides how to feel. Yes, this decision might be subconsciously made. And it is normally made rather quick for you. That again does not mean you need to keep running on automatic. You could overwrite your subconscious decisions at any time.

Everyone and everything around you has an impact on you. That is a fact. You could prove it by feeling into the energy of the situation or your living circumstances.

Yes, you could feel the energy as you are energy. Again everything around you has an impact on your energy. However, your energy is what has the most impact on you and your surroundings.

It is your energy, your feelings that have the most impact on your life. If someone or something makes you feel bad, it is that you decided to feel bad.

There isn't anything wrong with it, except when you start blaming others for your negative feelings. Nobody could give you a bad feeling, except you.

The Role Of The Environment And Why It Doesn't Matter

I know this is hard stuff. But one day you may see it for yourself and you take responsibility for your feelings. The good ones and the bad ones.

Also, the good feelings you experience are not given to you by anyone. You have them inside yourself. So why not use your natural ability and decide to feel good all the time.

Even if you have to make this decision a million times. Who cares? It's YOU who cares! You should care about how you feel. I assume you do whatever it takes to keep your body healthy and fit. That means getting some food and keeping it clean.

Am I right? I believe I am. Now, why don't you put as much effort into feeling good as you put into your body? It's your decision in the end anyway. Though you could keep going and allow all the world to pull you down or you decide to lift yourself up.

By lifting yourself up, you lift up everyone around you and maybe even more people than you could ever imagine.

Wherever you are in the world, under which circumstances, situations, or in which ever country you are living, it is only up to you to raise your energy. Don't wait for anyone to do it for you. No one can raise your energy except you.

Yes, others could help you by giving you a lift, but that could only be a starting point.

It is nice if others do something for you. I know, it really is.

Appreciate it as much as you could. If you drill deep enough you will find out, that there are things inside yourself no one else could change except you.

Don't be afraid. All these things are just memories in form of energy. And you are the highest energy of all. Why not use it for the good of yourself and everyone else? Sounds good? Great.

Let's do something together right now. Increase the Love you feel for yourself. You don't feel Love for yourself? I don't believe that. You do, but you are afraid to be told to be vain if you love yourself. That's weird.

Love never hurts. Love brings your life into harmony and that could be scary at times. However, keep on loving.

And in case you are afraid to get too proud about loving yourself, don't worry. If you love yourself pride does not have a chance.

That is because Love is much higher than Pride. The Love I mean here is unconditional, which is the true and only Love there is. Anything different than that is not Love. At least not from my point of view.

Let's go for it again. Love yourself a little bit more. And a bit more. And a bit more. Just allow love to flow through you.

The Role Of The Environment And Why It Doesn't Matter

What do you experience? Feeling better or worse? You might feel worse as somehow we all have a weird relationship with love. That means we resist accepting it for ourselves.

Or we do not accept love for ourselves when we haven't done something of value to receive it. Thus we feel not being good enough to be loved.

Honestly, it's not true that you need to be a certain way or do certain things to be worth receiving love.

Just go ahead and give love to yourself. Yes, right now. Invite the love to come up in yourself and observe what happens.

You could not force Love. Just allow and observe.

Hopefully, now you have a better understanding of why your environment or circumstances don't matter. You have the greatest impact on your world.

When you keep staying in high positive energy you will recognize that you have a much higher impact on your life experience than anyone else.

It is your decision that gives your environment or circumstances power over your experience.

If your environment or circumstances pull you down then it is because you place your attention on it constantly.

Focus your attention on what you want, on your positive energy. You are positive energy. Focus on Love.

Let's summarize the role of your environment and why it doesn't matter:

► Your Environment is everyone and everything around you. If you take an expansive perspective then your environment is the whole Universe.
► Your Environment is pointing you back to yourself. With everything you feel, you are reminded to look at yourself.
► Your Environment has an impact on your feelings as well as on your actions/reactions.
► You decide to stay at the energy level of your environment.
► You could decide to be positive or negative no matter what your environment energy level is.
► It's a subconscious habit to follow the energy level of our environment.
► By constantly repeating our decision to stay positive and loving we could even influence the energy level of our environment.
► You decide to be positive or negative. It is always your decision. You could be positive or negative, but not both at the same time.

How To Stay Above De-Energizing Environments And Circumstances

We all have had tough times. The year 2020 might have been one for you. Maybe you once lost your job or your money or even worst someone you love.

All these events have the potential to pull us down into being negative. It does not need to be this way. But it does not mean to neglect feelings of sadness, pain, or whatever you experience.

These feelings are part of our human experience. We could always recognize how we feel and decide if we like to feel this way.

Even at moments where it might not look possible to us to feel positive as the upcoming feelings are so strong, we could decide to be positive and loving.

It takes courage to allow the arising feelings to be and decide to let them go. To decide to feel more positive while bad things happening in your life takes practice.

At every moment you could use the four steps described in this book to change how you feel.

So far you have seen that your feelings are a reaction to what happens around you. Thus if you wouldn't be bothered by what is happening you wouldn't have any feelings about it.

Also, you have seen that you are the one who decides to go with a feeling or decides to feel different.

All of the above has a great impact on your life. Because now you might see that you are not the victim to your environment or circumstances.

The more you delve into negative feelings, the more negative things start happening in your life.

Well, what is true for negativity could only be true for positivity too.

We are living in a world of duality. You need to decide. You could have either this or that, but not both. You could not be negative and positive at the same time.

You could not be sad and laugh at the same time. You decide to experience one of the two.

That said I hope you already have a clue how to stay above down-pulling environments and circumstances.

Yes, you are right. You decide to stay above them mentally. Your power is your decision. Even if you need to decide a thousand times.

How long does it take for you to decide? Honestly, it takes a split-second.

The Role Of The Environment And Why It Doesn't Matter

When you decide, you decide. Done. There is no arguing about what, why, and how you decide or if there might be a better decision.

Just imagine weighing up if feeling positive is a good decision when you feel negative. Why would you decide for being negative? Does it feel nice to be negative? No, it doesn't. Though why not decide to be positive.

Again, you decide to stay above the down-pulling environment around you. Decide and decide and decide that your feelings are bigger than anything around you.

It's not about being superior. We are all equal. We all have access to the same high power that is inside of all of us. We have more in common than we have differences.

You do not need to agree to this right now. One day you might agree with me as you experience what I mean by the above.

As well you don't need to believe all the above. You could find out for yourself. You have to find out for yourself that all of this is true.

Because only if you find out for yourself, you know it. And knowing comes from experience that you are the energy, the power.

Yet, this real power that you are is very subtle. You might overlook it. It is subtle as true unconditional love is.

The same is true for water for example. Water could be so subtle and soft.

On the other hand, water could be so powerful and destructive you want to get out of its way as fast as you can.

The energy within you is similar to water. But even if it acts powerfully it might still be much more gentle than water. Don't be afraid. You could not harm yourself or others when you are lovingly using your high-energy potential.

You are using it anyway not being aware of it. That is because you are this energy. Notice it for yourself.

Where do you take your energy from? From inside of yourself, right? Could you feel into this energy a little bit more? And more? And more? And even more?

What do you experience? Whatever it is, let the feeling go. Relax and let go.

However, you feel lighter when you let go. And the lighter feeling shows you that you let go. That's how you prove it to yourself.

Even if I repeat myself, as a child you instinctively knew how to let go. It's a natural ability. While we grow up we forget about this natural ability.

This is how you stay above down-pulling environments and circumstances.

The Role Of The Environment And Why It Doesn't Matter

But let's recap, to have the big picture:

► by deciding to stay positive you could stay above down-pulling environments and circumstances.
► it may take some practice to stay positive all the time.
► it's always your decision which feeling you follow or if you chose a different one.
► You could only experience your feelings about your environment or circumstances.
► As the feelings you have about a situation are only yours, it's up to you to let these feelings go and decide to feel different.
► You are the power as you are the one who makes the decision.
► It is all about unconditional love. For yourself and others.
► Unconditional Love is a subtle but extremely powerful energy. You couldn't think it, you could only experience it.

The Less You Force It, The Easier It Becomes

Today we all want results fast. If we want something, we want it NOW! Patience seems to be a word from ages past. In case we don't get what we want immediately we lose interest or get angry.

Neither of these reactions is helping us to feel good about ourselves. The more you force something, the more it feels you get away from it. Therefore you force things even more.

And the more you force it the more effort you need to take to make it happen. It's the total opposite of how it really works.

The less you force anything, the easier things become. Forcing could also mean that you force yourself to do something you need to do but don't like to do.

Not liking to do the thing makes you force yourself to do it and it takes lots of energy. When you decide to do it and allow it to be easy, things might happen easier than you think.

The Less You Force It, The Easier It Becomes

And we all have things we need to do which we don't like. We have to do them anyway. Though, why not make it as easy as possible.

Sometimes willpower could stand in the way for us to get things done. Willpower is not good and not bad.

You and I just have to get aware of how we use our willpower and to which level we put it into something. More willpower does not mean that things work out better.

Depending on the things you like to do or achieve it might be enough to put only a bit of willpower into it. Just enough willpower to keep you going.

Here willpower could also mean a decision which you have made with full determination. You are determined to achieve your goal.

Yet you are not forcing your goal into existence. Yes, I know it sounds weird. Just imagine you want something to work out badly. Feels somewhat powerful and also there is some uncertainty about really making it happen.

When you relax and focus on the result and allow things to happen, you put much more concentrated and higher energy into the result. This may even feel less exhausting.

The feeling of uncertainty/doubt, if you can make it happen, is kind of normal. But that does not mean it has to be that way.

When you get to the right level of determination and energy you put into something, you come to a point where you know that it will happen. You could not force good things to happen to you constantly. You have to allow good things to happen to you constantly.

To achieve this, all you have to do is to concentrate on the things happening inside of yourself. Your feelings and thoughts are the things you need to observe.

Wait! Please do not try to force your feelings and thoughts in a specific direction. Decide!

Deciding is much more powerful than forcing a change. Decisions are made in a split second again and again. Forcing something to change is putting energy into it permanently, which is not necessary. The latter could be exhausting.

Be smart – Decide!

You might indeed succeed by putting a lot of energy into what you want to achieve or change. But is that smart? I don't think so.

The less energy you need to achieve something the better. Yes, sometimes it might be needed to put more effort into something. However, that does not mean you have to do it all the time. It is a good habit to observe yourself and recognize when you start pushing things to happen from inside. Relax and focus on the End Result you like to achieve.

Then move on. Do what needs to be done, but do it with and from Love.

If you can't feel Love and/or Joy while doing something, just smile and you might feel much better about it.

Remember, you need to decide. You could either be smiling and be happy or disapproving and feeling bad. But you can't do both at the same time.

Let's summarize:

▶ We all want results fast if not immediately.
▶ Patience seems to be a word of the past.
▶ We are constantly pushing for results.
▶ Using pure willpower is not always the best decision.
▶ Making a firm decision might be even more powerful than using pure willpower alone.
▶ Willpower is used to keep yourself focused on your End Result and not to make the End Result happen.

How To Stick With Your Decision To Stay In High Energy

You may wonder, but it needs your decision to stay in high energy. And it takes your observation to see if you drift away.

In case you drift away from the higher energy, you have to decide again to feel better. Thus it is a continuous process of monitoring where you are at the moment.

But wait, this may sound like a lot of work. It may is at the start. With time you get used to being aware of how you feel and could direct yourself into higher energy.

The process to stay in high energy is simple either. It only takes your internal observation and a decision.

I guess the latter one is something you already expected. Yes, it always comes down to your decision.

Just a quick reminder. It is not about suppressing any feelings or thoughts. Allow them to be. They are just energy.

The moment you recognize you feel bothered or negative about something is the moment you need to decide to be positive and loving.

Sure, you have to repeat the decision again and again, but it's a fast process. Deciding just takes a second or less. Thus you could do it easily and fast as often as you need to.

It's enough to decide to be positive and loving every time you recognize you are negative. With time you become more present to your feelings and thoughts as well as to your higher energy.

Repetition is how things are learned and improved.

To sum up again:

▶ Observing your thoughts and feelings helps you to recognize when you drift away from positive high energy.
▶ Allow negative feelings and thoughts to be.
▶ Making a decision is how you stay in higher energy.
▶ Repetition is key. Decide again and again until you feel the higher energy.
▶ Use the Process described in the chapter "How To Get Into High Energy In 4 Simple Steps" starting on page 51.

How An Accountability Partner Could Help You To Increase Your Energy

Sometimes it is a good thing if there is someone around us who could point us in the right direction. This is true about staying in higher energy too. In case you go down into negative energy others might recognize it earlier than we do ourselves.

Though if you have someone who knows you well and is willing to point out, that you do not sound positive, that might be helpful.

Your partner must know that this is not to be used to disapprove of you if you drift into negativity. That would be counterproductive. It's also not about forcing you to suppress your feelings.

Therefore it makes sense to find someone who likes to stay in high energy as well. Then you both could remind each other about staying in high energy.

Furthermore, it may not be a good idea to select a family member. This is because we are much more triggered by family members than by other people.

A very good friend of yours might be the best choice for you. However, having an accountability partner is not a requirement. The only thing that is required is your decision and determination.

Yes, it's again your decision that counts.

How To Stick With Your Decision To Stay In High Energy

In case you decide to have and find an accountability partner, you might find out that it is a bit easier to stay in higher energy.

This is because the higher energy is contagious. Therefore if two or more people come together with high energy or the intent to improve their energy level the lifting is a bit easier.

Don't get me wrong, it is not a necessity to have a partner. You could get in higher energy and stay there by yourself.

Sometimes it could still be a good idea to have a partner. I guess you got my point. Even if you have a partner you do not need to depend on each other.

It's a loose bond. You meet when one or both of you need it.

And as you already know it doesn't take much time to get into higher energy.

But how would you do this when you have a partner? Well, one could guide the other by leading through the 4-Step process.

It is that easy. Like to have it even easier? I guessed that.

You could just use Step 4. Yes, ask the other one which feeling he/she likes to feel and decide to feel that way.

For example, your partner might want to feel more joy. Ask your partner to allow joy to come up? Allow more joy to come up? Could you allow even more joy to come up?

And so on. Your partner could confirm the question with yes or say nothing and just observer. Either way works. Of course, answering is better if you work together over the phone. Thus each of you knows that the other one is still using the process.

Do you know what we do now? Yes, we sum up again:

▶ A partner could remind you to stay in higher positive energy
▶ Choose a partner from outside your family as family members could trigger you much more than others.
▶ A partner could help you to get into positive high energy easier.
▶ You do not need a partner, but sometimes it could help.

30-Second-Method To Stop Overwhelm Or Any Other Feeling

It is a good thing to know how to get yourself out of a bad mood rather quickly.

Even if you might have to repeat the process multiple times until you feel getting into higher energy.

Here is a simple 30-Second-Method to help you get out of a strong feeling:

▶ take a deep breath in
▶ exhale slowly
▶ repeat slow and deep breathing at least two more times

You could do anything you want – but please do something positive. Even if you would jump around or solve a mathematic equation. It would help. Why?

Because it takes your thinking and feeling away from the overwhelm or any other feelings you have and don't like.

This is not to say that the overwhelming feeling will be gone. This method just allows you to get back in control.

From being more in control you could then practice the simple four-step process described earlier. Using deep breathing has several positive effects.

First, it helps you to calm down. Second, it provides you with more oxygen which is good for your body anyway. Third, it directs your mind away from the thing that bothers you.

And at last, it helps you to let go of the feeling as you are becoming more relaxed.

When you are tense you could not let go of a feeling. You are too busy holding on to it or trying to avoid it. Only if you relax, you could let the feeling dissolve.

Experiencing strong feelings that make you feel tense, it's similar to a dog being out of control and not reacting to anything.

No matter what you shout at the dog, the dog will continue being out of control. But if you get the dog distracted from what it is doing at the moment, it may calm down and you are in control.

The same happens to us in overwhelm or any other strong feeling. No one could tell you to relax.

Your mind is too much occupied with the thing that caused the overwhelm. Taking the mind off-track to something different like breathing deep allows you to get in control again.

As said it has so many more benefits. It may even take less than 30 seconds for you to get the mind off track.

It just takes one second. The moment you start a deep breath is where you decided to be done with the overwhelm.

Furthermore, deep breathing could be done in any situation. No one around you may even notice it.

Do you recognize something here, that we have been talking about all the time in the previous chapters? Yes? What is it? Yes, you are right. Again it is all about your decision.

You decide to calm down and get your mind off track.

You see, your decisions are a powerful tool. A decision you have made will run until you decide to stop or change it.

It is similar to a program on your computer. You start the program with a decision and it keeps running until you close the program. It may run in the background while you are not using it.

The same is true for your decisions. Decide carefully and delete the decisions you do not like to run anymore.

How to delete old decisions? The moment you are aware of an old decision you just decide to drop it. That's all.

Here is the summary again:

► Take a deep breath or do anything to break through any strong intense feeling.
► Your decision is what makes the difference. You decide to be calm.
► Deep breathing has several positive side effects.
► Delete old decisions by deciding to drop them.

Is There a 'Downside' To High Energy?

You may wonder why being in High Energy or to Feel Great could have a Downside. Well, we live in a World of Duality, thus there are always two sides to a coin.

While it is a great thing for you and the people around you to stay in high energy and feeling great, there might be people who do not like it.

Though, the downside is, that some people will not like to be or stay with you, if your energy is high. And that could even be people of your family. As already mentioned in the chapter about Environment, we try to pull down everyone around us, if we have the feeling they might rise above us.

This mostly happens because of a subconscious habit we all have. We all like to be the Best, the Winner. We do not like to be not as good as others. It's not personal. It has nothing to do with you. It is just a habit. You could see it in yourself when you observe yourself a little bit.

Is There a 'Downside' To High Energy?

However, it is not a good idea to depend your well-being and happiness on anything or any person.

The more you love the more you will have the people around you which you like to spend time with and which like to spend time with you.

Another downside could be that you are trying to ignore any negative feeling you may have. That's not gonna work in the long run.

Staying in high energy does not mean preventing negative feelings and thoughts from coming up.

It is much better to use your higher energy level to allow the negative feelings and thoughts and let them go.

You may find out by doing the above that your energy is getting even higher.

And don't wonder when your life starts to get better or worse. If it is getting worse, you need to keep going as there is a clean-up happening.

It is like sorting out old stuff. You just give away or throw away the things you do not need anymore.

That also happens while you are increasing your energy.

And of course, your life will get better at one point, if you keep going and doing the work described in this book.

Don't blame anyone if you stop and things stay the same as before. It is all your decision. You probably knew I was going to say that again.

You decide. Just do it consciously and in a direction, you like things to go.

Are you afraid now? I could understand that. We never know what will happen in our life, when we decide to do something or not.

Life itself is uncertainty. Only one thing is certain – one day your body will die. Anything else is uncertain.

We all try so hard to make our life more certain and secure.

The highest certainty and security you could ever have is found within yourself. You do not need to believe that right now.

Practice the 4-Steps and find out for yourself.

There might be more downsides but none is coming to my mind right now.

The upsides are much more than the downsides. The above is what you need to be aware of.

Is There a 'Downside' To High Energy?

That said, let's recap:

- ▶ Not everyone might like when you are in higher energy and feel great.
- ▶ We all try to pull others down if we feel they are better than us. It's not personal.
- ▶ Even family members might not want you to improve.
- ▶ The more your energy is shifting into higher and higher energy there might be things and/or people leaving your life. It's just cleaning up your life. Keep going until it is getting better.

Now What?

Hopefully you enjoyed reading this book and had fun doing the exercises. Whatever your experiences had been, my wish for you is that you have the courage and persistence to keep going with using the exercises in your daily life.

To keep up your efforts, you could make it a regular habit. The more often you do the exercises I described the better you may feel.

Feeling better is just the start of your journey. The better you feel, the more positive energy you send out, the better your life may become.

I could not guarantee that to you. Because it is up to you to do what is necessary. I couldn't make you feel better, I couldn't improve your life, I could only show you how to do it yourself.

Though there are things you could do for yourself to make it work for you. Here are some ideas:

Now What?

- ▶ Set aside time for yourself every day. A few minutes may do it as a start.
- ▶ Observe what you feel.
- ▶ Recognize if you are trying to force feeling good/love.
- ▶ Accept Love for yourself.
- ▶ Accept Love and Peace for everyone.
- ▶ Have some stillness once in a while or more often, whenever you feel you need it.

If you would like to have some more assistance, you may sign-up for a free membership on my website.

In case you like this book and it helped you, I really appreciate it if you take the time and write a review through the place where you bought it.

Or you send a testimonial as well as any questions or suggestions you have to: books@s2executivecoaching.com

CONGRATULATIONS for having read this book and starting yourself on a wonderful journey.

I wish you all the Best in Life and lots of Love.

Best Regards,
Stephan

Acknowledgments

This section is to say thank you. Thank you to all the people that have had an impact on me and my journey.

That includes you as well. As without you reading this book, there would be something missing.

Of course, I'm grateful for the support from my relatives, friends, and many other people (that includes you again). I really feel blessed.

Thanks to Life and Love as well for enabling me to be on an amazing journey that keeps reminding me about who I really am.

I'm grateful for the possibility to be on this journey and for everyone I come across who has helped me so far. It had been too many people already to list all their names here.

So, THANK YOU, to every one of you.

If you enjoyed **Feel Great: It's Your Decisions!** you may also like...

Focus Yourself And Get Things Done

Are you tired of the "Always-Busy-Trap"? Then this Report about a Focus Exercise could be what you need.
A simple yet effective method to focus yourself on what you want.

You could download it for free when you are a member of
www.s2executivecoaching.com

An Audio of a guided Focus exercise is available for members as well.

Exercise Quick Reference:

The exercises start or could be found on the pages referenced below.